Law Sch

Business Organizations Outline

Green Ribbon Engagements, LLC

2015

Outline is keyed to the Hamilton, Macey, & Moll, Corporations Including Partnerships and Limited Liability Companies, Cases & Materials, West Publishing, Eleventh Edition, (2010), and Statutory Supplement by Robert Hamilton and Jonathan Macey, American Casebook Series, Eleventh Edition (2010).

Disclaimer:

All rights reserved. No part of this publication may be reproduced, distributed, or transmitted in any form or by any means, including photocopying, recording, or other electronic or mechanical methods, without the prior written permission of the publisher, except in the case of brief quotations embodied in critical reviews and certain other noncommercial uses permitted by copyright law.

Note from the editor:

Thank you for purchasing our Business Organizations Outline. Enclosed, you will find a raw outline meant to save you time while enhancing your understanding of Business Organizations. This raw outlines covers a clear and concise introduction to sole proprietorships, general partnerships, joint ventures, limited partnerships, the hybrids (limited liability partnerships (LLP), limited liability limited partnerships (LLLP), and limited liability companies (LLC), corporations, and agency principles. This is a great study tool and resource as it covers the black letter law and case law for your exam in a concise fashion to help save you time and maximize your grade on your final exam.

Best of luck in your coursework and legal careers!

Now go out there and book your Business Organizations class!

Business Organizations Outline

A. **Agency Principles**
   - **Agency Defined: Rest (3d) of Agency § 1.01:**
     - Agency is the fiduciary relationship that arises when one person (a "principal") manifests assent to another person (an "agent") that the agent shall act on the principal's behalf and subject to the principal's control, and the agent manifests assent or otherwise consents so to act.
   - **Agent:**
     - The person acting for another.
     - **Rest. 3d Agency § 8.01 General Fiduciary Principle:**
       - An agent has a fiduciary duty to act loyally for the principal's benefit in all matters connected with the agency relationship.
   - **Principal:**
     - The person for whom the agent is acting.
   - **Elements of Agency:**
     - **(1)** The manifestation by the principal that the agent shall act for him,
     - **(2)** The agent's acceptance of the undertaking,
     - **(3)** The understanding of the parties that the principal is to be in control of the undertaking
   - **Types of Agencies:**
     - **Disclosed Principal/Disclosed Agent**
       - At the time of the agent's transactions, the third party has notice that the third party is acting for a principal and has notice of the principal's identity.
     - **Partially Disclosed**
       - At the time of the agent's transaction, the third party has notice that the agent is or may be acting for a principal, but also no notice of the principal's identity.

- o **Undisclosed/Non-disclosed Principal Agency**
  - If at the time of the agent's transaction, the third party has no notice that the agent is acting for a principal.
- **Types of Authorities:**
  - o **1. Actual:**
    - Arises from the manifestation to an agent that the agent has power to deal with others as a representative of the principal...binding the principal.
    - **2 types of Actual Authority:**
    - **a. Express:**
      - Oral or written statements proven to the satisfaction of the courts.
    - **b. Implied:**
      - Inferred from the principal's prior acts.
        - o **Incidental authority:**
          - Authority to do incidental acts related to the transaction that is authorized.
  - o **2. By Law & Equity/Apparent/Inherent/Estoppel:**
    - Apparent and estoppel (reliance) arises from the manifestation of a principal to a third party that another person is authorized to act as an agent for the principal.
    - This flows from the principal to the third party.
    - **Burden of Proof:**
      - 1. There was a principal/agent relationship
      - 2. The agent was acting within the scope of the authority allocated.
      - 3. The contract was created between the third party and the principal.
      - 4. The principal acted negligently.

- 3. **Ratification:**
  - This is retroactive authority.
  - This depends on the behavior of the principal.
  - The principal accepts an agents unauthorized transaction as valid and establishes a course of action consistent with acceptance.

B. **Types of Business Organizations**
- **Sole Proprietorship**
  - Business owned by a single person
  - No legal requirements to become a sole proprietorship
  - There is no requirement for filing if the person is using his or her own name.
  - However, if a person is using a different name than their first name, then there is a requirement for filing.
- **General (Ordinary) Partnership & Joint Venture**
  - A partnership is an entity distinct from its partners.
  - An association of 2 or more persons to carry on as co-owners a business for profit does not require a filing of an organizational document with the state.
  - All partners in a general partnership have a right to participate in the management of the business.
  - The law imposes unlimited personal liability on partners for the obligations of the partnership.
- **Limited Partnership**
  - A partnership comprised of 2 classes of partners, general and limited, that is formed by filing an organizational document with the state.
  - General partners have unlimited personal liability for the ventures obligations.
- **The Corporation**
  - A corporation is viewed as a separate legal entity whose identity is distinct from that of its owners

(known as "shareholders").
- File the articles of incorporation with the secretary of the state.
  - **Closely Held**
    - Business with relative few owners, whose ownership interests are not publically traded on an established market.
  - **Publicly Held**
    - Business that has a large number of owners with ownership interests that are routinely bought and sold on a public market.
- **The Hybrids**
  - **Limited Liability Partnership (LLP)**
    - Limited partners have limited liability for the ventures obligations.
  - **Limited Liability Limited Partnership (LLLP)**
    - A limited partnership that provides an "LLP like" limited liability protection to some or all of the partners.
  - **Limited Liability Company (LLC)**
    - The preferred business form, formed by required state filing.
    - A legal entity that is separate and distinct from its owners, known as members.

C. **General (Ordinary) Partnership**
- **Formation:**
  - **DO NOT HAVE TO REGISTER A PARTNERSHIP WITH THE STATE.**
  - Partnership results from contract either express or implied.
    - But the best way to form a partnership is through a written (express) contract.

- - But if a partnership is made orally, then it is based on the objective test of a reasonable person.
    - Under implied partnerships, and if there is no contract, then the court will look to the behavior of the parties to see
    - **RUPA § 101(6):** Partnership means an association of 2 or more persons carry on as co-owners a business for profit.
    - **RUPA § 203 Partnership Property:** Property acquired by a partnership is property of the partnership and NOT the property of the partners individually.
- **Liability:**
    - The partners of the partnership have unlimited personal liability.
    - Partners are jointly and severally liable for obligations of the partnership.
    - **Principal Agency Relationship:**
        - The partners of the partnership are agents of the partnership.
        - The partnership is the principal.
        - A partner confers agency upon each partner
        - Every partner in combination with the other partners is the principal.
- **Internal Universe:**
    - The partnership
    - The court will be able to determine what the principal and agent agreed upon by their conduct.
- **External Universe:**
    - Third party
    - The third party must show reasonable reliance upon the acts of the internal universe (the partnership).
- **Profit/Losses:**
    - **Profit:**

- Court will look to the partnership contract to see how profits are divided upon partners.
- However, if the contract is silent, then profits will be divided equally among the partners—**RUPA § 401(b).**
    - **Losses:**
        - Court will look to the partnership contract to see how losses are divided upon partners.
        - However, if the contract is silent, then losses will be divided equally among the partners—**RUPA § 401(b).**
    - **Stated Profits/Silent Losses:**
        - However, if the contract speaks to profits but is silent on losses, then the profits will be divided based on contract and the losses will be split equally.
    - **Silent Profits/Stated Losses:**
        - If the contract is silent on profits and expressly speaks to losses, then the partnership profit division will be split equally and the losses will be divided by what is expressed in the contract.
- **Voting:**
    - Unless there is an agreement to the contrary, each partner casts an equal vote regardless of equitable interests.
- **Ownership Interests:**
    - **RUPA § 201(a):** Property acquired by a partnership is property of the partnership and not of the partners individually.
- **Fiduciary Duty:**
    - Partners owe each other the highest loyalty, and must disclose opportunities that arise in order for both to have an equal chance to take advantage of it.
    - **RUPA § 301: Partner Agent of Partnership:**

- Each partner is an agent of the partnership for the purposes of the business UNLESS the party had no authority.
- An execution of an instrument (i.e., a contract) in the partnership's name binds the partnership.
- UNLESS, the partner had no authority to act for the partnership in the particular matter and the person with whom the partner was dealing KNEW or had received notification that the partner lacked authority.
  - **RUPA § 303: Statement of Partnership Authority:**
    - A partnership MAY file a statement of partnership authority to the state.
    - It is permissible and NOT mandatory.
    - The contract that is stated in § 301 is binding on the partnership over anything filed with the State under § 303.
    - If a § 303 is NOT filed, then each partner is agent of the partnership for the purpose of partnership business, and each partner is an agent under § 1.01 Rest. 3d of Agency and each agent owes a fiduciary duty to the partnership.
  - **Is a fiduciary duty a one-way street or a 2-way street? Does the principal owe a fiduciary duty to the agent?**
    - **No this is a one-way street, the principal does NOT owe a fiduciary duty to the agent.**
  - **Duty of Care:**
    - A partner owes a fiduciary duty to the partnership, but once an partner leaves the partnership, the fiduciary duty is terminated.
  - **Management & Operation:**

- - - Each partner has an equal right to the management of the business, and any business performed under the scope of the partnership can be breached or violated by majority of the partners.
    - **RUPA § 401(j):** A difference arising as to a matter in the ordinary course of business of a partnership may be decided by a majority of the partners. An act outside of the ordinary course of business of a partnership or an amendment to the partnership agreement may be undertaken ONLY with the consent of ALL of the members.
    - **RUPA § 401(i):** A person may become a partner only with the consent of all the partners. An individual partner is not entitled to add more partners UNLESS the contract provided for it in a written contract agreement.
  - **Personal Property:**
    - Each one of the partners of the partnership owns their own PP.
    - **RUPA § 502:** The property of the partnership is owned by the partnership.
    - **Partner's Rights to Property:**
      - Rights in specific partnership property
      - Interest in the partnership.
      - Right to participate in the management.
- **Types of Durational Partnerships:**
  - **At will:**
    - A partnership where the partners have not specified any definite term or particular undertaking for the partnership.
    - Partners in an at will partnership have the freedom to expel another partner if the

offending partner damages the personal confidence and trust of the partnership.
- A party in a partnership at will is entitled to give notice to the partnership, this dissolves the partnership.
- **For a Term:**
  - It is a partnership where the partners have agreed, explicitly or implicitly, that the partnership shall have a definite term or a particular undertaking.
  - **Expressed:**
    - Most potent way of creating a partnership is though an express, written contract specifically stating the term of the partnership agreement.
  - **Implied:**
    - Duration is implied (written or verbal) by:
      - Creating the partnership for a specific task, which implies the time it takes to complete the task.
      - The partnership entering into an obligation, which implies the time required to satisfy those obligations (lease, mortgage, etc).

- **Assignment of a Partner's Interest:**
  - 1. Always check the contract to make sure whether the partner can assign his or her interest in the partnership.
  - 2. Assigning an interest to a third party assignee does not dissolve the partnership.
  - 3. The assignee has a right to receive the partner's share of the profits.

- 4. The assignee has no right in management nor a right to inspect books.
- Under § 404(i), a person may become a partner only with the consent of all partners OR if under contract law, one partner can allowed to vote in new partners without the consent of the other partners.
- **Ending the Partnership:**
  - **Dissolution:** Partners always have the POWER to cause dissolution BUT may not have the legal right (i.e., they may have liability in law or equity).
  - **RUPA § 601: Events Causing a Partner's Dissociation:**
    - **(1)** The partnership's having notice of the partner's express will to withdraw as a partner or on a later date specified by the partner;
    - **(2)** An event agreed to in the partnership agreement as causing the partner's dissociation;
    - **(3)** The partner's expulsion pursuant to the partnership agreement;
    - **(4)** The partner's expulsion by the unanimous vote of the other partners if:
      - **(i)** It is unlawful to carry on on the partnership business with that partner; or
      - **(ii)** There has been a transfer of all or substantially all of that partner's transferable interest in the partnership.
    - **(NON-BREACH) Alternative 1:** The court will order a dissolution, a winding up, or a termination of the business.
      - If the partnership agreement has not run its course, and the two parties no

longer get along, the parties could ask the court for a dissolution of the partnership.
- **RUPA § 801(2)(ii):** A partnership is dissolved, and its business must be wound up, only upon the occurrence of any of the following events, and it is the express will of all of the partners to wind up the partnership business.
  - This is NOT a breach of contract.
    - **(BREACH) Alternative 2:** Expel this breaching partner, allow the innocent party to determine who the new partner is for the partnership business.
    - **(BREACH) Alternative 3:** The innocent party would be asking the court to dissociate the breaching party from the partnership so that breaching party would be expelled from the partnership.
    - **Rule of law:** A partner does not have the right to dissolve the partnership when his conduct is the only conduct that is adversely affecting the business.
    - The innocent party would be working with **RUPA § 601(5):**
      - The partner is dissociated from a partnership upon the occurrence of either of these events:
        - 1. The partner engaged in wrongful conduct that adversely and materially affected the partnership business;
        - 2. The partner willfully or

- persistently committed a material breach;
  - 3. The partner engaged in a conduct relating to the partnership business which makes it not reasonably practicable to carry on the business in the partnership with the partner.
- If the court agreed with Lewis, then the court will order the innocent party to buyout the breaching party under **RUPA § 701(a)**.
  - **The Buyout Process:**
    - **Step 1:**
      - Determine the buyout price under RUPA § 701(a).
      - The court will determine what the buyout price is and it would do an accounting (calculation) to determine what the assets are valued out based on GAAP (Generally Accepted Accounting Principles).
      - You will value the assets by appointing an

- appraisal or more.
- The partnership assets would be appraised since the partnership business is not being sold.
- The value of the assets would be (X) and the liabilities (Y) would be subtracted. (X)–(Y).
- The difference is the partnership value.
- Ordinarily, this will be divided based on the partnership agreement or under RUPA § 807 (equally between the partners).
    - **Step 2:**
        - The damages are next divided by the court.
        - If the damages for the breach of contract is $4 million, and we know that the

total value is at $5 million and $2.5 million is going to be divided equally among the partners, the breaching party is going to have to pay $1.5 million out of pocket to meet his $4 million breaching price.

D. Limited Partner:
- A limited partnership is comprised of at least one general partner and at least one limited partner.
- **RUPA § 201(11):** The limited partnership is considered a general entity.
- General partner has unlimited personal liability for the obligations of the firm.
- Limited partner has NO liability for the debts of the venture beyond the loss of his investment.
- **Formation:**
    - LP CAN ONLY be formed by filing a certificate of limited partnership with the secretary of state of the appropriate jurisdiction, and it requires:
        - (1) The name of the LP
        - (2) The identity of the general partners.
    - **Partnership Agreement:**
        - Details the rights and duties of the partners and the overall operation.
- **Management & Operation:**
    - **RULPA § 403(a):** A general partner in an LP have the same rights and powers as a general partner in a general partnership.

- The general partner's right and powers include:
  - 1. The ability to participate in management;
  - 2. The ability to bind the partnership via apparent authority;
  - 3. The ability to vote (NOT limited partners, limited partners CANNOT vote).
    - **Control Rule:**
      - A limited partner can lose her limited liability protection if she participates in the control of the business.
- **Fiduciary Duties:**
  - **General Partners:**
    - Directors of a corporate general partner owe a fiduciary duty to a limited partnership.
    - **Plain Talk:**
      - A general partner in a general ordinary partnership and a general partner in a limited partnership BOTH owe their respective partnerships a fiduciary duty. Both partners have unlimited personal liability.
  - **Limited Partners:**
    - Limited partners do not have the power to withdraw during an agreed term.
    - Limited partner is NOT liable for the obligations of an LP, UNLESS he participates in the control of the business.
      - Having the right to participate expressly written into the LP contract does NOT constitute participation in management unless the limited partner exercises that right.
    - If the limited partner does not participate in the control of the business, he is liable on to persons who transact business with the LP

reasonably believing the limited partner was a general partner due to the limited partner's conduct.
- **Dissociation & Dissolution:**
  - **Dissociation:**
    - A general partner may withdraw at any time by giving written notice to the other partners.
    - BUT, if the withdrawer violates the partnership agreement, the LP may recover damages.
    - **Types of Dissociation:**
      - **Type 1 Wrongful Dissociation:**
        - Breach of contract
        - Damages can be awarded
      - **Type 2 Rightful Dissociation:**
        - Would be in accordance with the partnership agreement, and would not be a breach.
        - A general ordinary partner may willfully dissociate himself of herself.
  - **Dissolution:**
    - An LP is dissolved upon:
      - 1. At the time specified in the certificate of limited partnership;
      - 2. Upon the occurrence of events specified in a written partnership agreement;
      - 3. Upon written consent of all partners;
      - 4. Upon an event of withdrawal of a general partner;
      - 5. By the entry of a decree of judicial dissolution.
- **D. Limited Liability Partnership (LLP)(HYBRID)**
  - An LLP is a general partnership that, depending upon the relevant statute, provides the partners with limited liability

for the firm's tort obligations or for both its tort and contract obligations.
- All of the partners have a right to participate in the management of the venture without risking a loss of their limited liability.
- **Differences between an LP and an LLP:**
    - 1. General ordinary partners—every partner is liable.
    - 2. An LP is comprised of at least one general partner (binding) and one limited partner (NOT binding).
    - 3. An LLP is a type of general partnership. The partners are NOT personally liable for the obligations of the partnership RULPA § 306(c). This LLP is a partial shield, the LLP has NO limited partners.
- **The Shield of Limited Liability:**
    - All partners have the benefits, responsibilities, and potential liabilities of general partners except that partners have no responsibilities for malpractice claims or for liabilities arising from negligence or misconduct, in which they are not personally involved.
- **Formation:**
    - Requires an association of 2 or more persons to carry on as co-owners a business or profit.
    - **First, an LLP is required to file a document with the secretary of state or other designated official.**
        - This must include:
            - 1. The firm's name
            - 2. The firm's address
            - 3. Statement of its business or purpose.

- o Second, some jurisdictions require an LLP to provide a specified amount of liability insurance.
E. **Limited Liability Limited Partnership (LLLP)(HYBRID)**
    - A general partner in an LLLP is liable for the obligations of the business only when the general partner in an LP would be liable.
    - In an LLLP, there are limited partners.
    - In an LLP, there are NOT limited partners.
    - The LLLP is associated with the LP.
    - The LLLP is a hybrid of the LP.
    - **Differences between a LLLP and LP:**
        - o A general partner in a LLLP are NOT personally liable for the torts of the other partners. A general partner will still be liable subject to unlimited personal liability. If the general partner in a LLLP has not exercised control or supervision over the general partners, the general partner will avoid liability.
F. **Limited Liability Company (LLC)(HYBRID)**
    - An LLC is a non-corporate business structure that provides its owners, known as members, with a number of benefits.
    - An LLC is an entity/person.
    - **Formation:**
        - o There must be an articles of incorporation filed with the secretary of the state.
        - o **Operating Agreement:**
            - A non-public document that resembles a contract, in which a general ordinary partnership is based on, namely third parties will not know what is in the operating agreement.
            - Must contain specifics of the rights and duties of all its members.

- There is no per se agency difference from a general ordinary partnership.
- Freedom of contract is the central to the LLC structure.
- If the operating agreement is silent as to inspection and information rights, the court uses statutory interpretation.
- **Management & Operation:**
    - **Two Types of General Governance:**
        - **1. Member-Managed:**
            - This is the default resembling a general partnership.
            - Each member has rights that resembles partners in a general ordinary partnership.
            - **RULLCA § 407(b)(1–5):** the management and conduct of the company is vested in its members.
            - In most statutes, members possess "partnership-like" authority to bind the LLC, and managers in a Manager-Managed LLCs have similar authority.
        - **2. Manager-Managed:**
            - This closely resembles a corporation.
            - **RULLCA § 407(c)(1–4)**
            - Members usually have NO statutory authority to bind the venture.
- **Inspection & Information Rights:**
    - A member of an LLC needs to have access to all the information a member might need to find out what is going on in the LLC.

- o You need to permit the members to have access to records to the LLC.
- o Statutes regulate how much access a participant in the business organization has.
- o Access depends on whether or not the LLC is member-managed or manager-managed.
- o A member in a member-managed LLC has more access to what is going on in the LLC. However, the courts and legislature do NOT permit a member to have access to everything. The burden of proof falls on the member to show the production of documents is NOT unreasonable.
    - **The balance is determined upon:**
        - 1. Statutes
        - 2. The operating agreement.
- **Entity Status:**
    - o RULLCA § 104(a): An LLC is explicitly characterized as a separate legal entity, whose identity is distinct from that of its owners.
    - o Where the owner retains essentially the same ownership interests in the property he has had prior to the conveyance, with plans to develop the property by improving it, with the possibility of future gains or losses, and can prevent the record owner from encumbering the property without his permission, such a transaction is NOT a sale or exchange.
- **Limited Liability:**
    - o The LLC provides its owners with limited liability for its venture's obligations.
    - o **RULLCA § 304(a):** A member or manager is NOT personally liable for debt, obligation, or liability of the company solely by reason of being or acting as a member or manager.

- If a person makes material representations to induce a purchaser to purchaser a parcel of land at a price far above FMV; and thereafter, forms an LLC to purchase and hold land, that person CANNOT later claim his status as an LLC member protects him from liability to the purchaser.
- **Fiduciary Duties:**
    - Minority shareholders owe majority shareholders a duty of loyalty to inform them in advance of any plans for a merger or a structure of a merger.
    - Fiduciary duties are more strict in a member-managed LLC than in a manager-managed LLC.
    - The court will look at the operating agreement to determine what level the member owes.
    - The majority owner has the power to remove and replace the manager appointed.
- **Ownership Interests & Transferability:**
    - The only transferrable interest in a LLC is personal property.
    - An ownership in an LLC entitles a member to:
        - **1. Financial Rights:**
            - Receive distributions and share in the profits and losses of the venture and;
        - **2. Management Rights:**
            - The right to participate in management and control of the business.
    - **Default rule:** an LLC member cannot transfer his full ownership interests.
- **Dissociation & Dissolution:**

- A member dissociates from a venture upon the occurrence of specified acts (example: withdrawal, resignation, death, or bankruptcy).
- **RULLCA § 601(a):** A member of an LLC may escape the grasp of an LLC by way of the operating agreement or statute. (A member has a right to dissociate either rightfully or wrongfully).
- The operating agreement may state how a withdrawn member gets their PP.
- **Regulatory Issues:**
  - A LLC cannot appear or conduct business in court without representation or representation by counsel.
  - An LLC is an entity and an artificial person.

G. Corporations
- **Formation:**
  - File Articles of Incorporation directly with the Secretary of the State.
  - **MBCA § 2.02: Articles of Incorporation (Constitution):**
    - **(a) The articles of incorporation must set forth:**
      - **(1)** A corporate name for the corporation that satisfies the requirements of section 4.01;
      - **(2)** The number of shares the corporation is authorized to issue;
      - **(3)** The street address of the corporation's initial registered office and the name of its initial registered agent at that office; and
      - **(4)** The name and address of each incorporator.
  - **MBCA § 2.05: Organization of Corporation:**
    - **(a) After incorporation:**

- **Alternative 1:** If the initial directors are named in the articles of incorporation, the initial directors shall hold an organizational meeting, at the call of the majority of the directors (quarum) to complete corporation by appointing officers, adopting bylaws, and carrying on any other business brought before the meeting.
- **Alternative 2:** If the initial directors are NOT named in the articles, the incorporator or incorporators SHALL hold an organizational meeting at the call of a majority of the incorporators:
  - **(i) to elect directors and complete the organization of the corporation; or**
  - **(ii) to elect a board of directors who SHALL complete the organization of the corporation.**
- Corporation is a person, born where the Secretary of State files the Articles of Incorporation.
- Once born, the corporation cannot function until it has directors.
- 100% of corporate powers SHALL be exercised (by or under the board)
- **Bylaws (federal statutes)**
  - Subservient to the Articles of Incorporation
  - **MBCA § 2.06: Bylaws:**
    - **(a)** The incorporators or board of directors of a corporation shall adopt initial bylaws for the corporation.
    - **(b)** The bylaws of a corporation may contain any provision for managing the business and regulating the

affairs of the corporation that is not inconsistent with law or the articles of incorporation.
- **Officers:**
  - **Secretary:**
    - The corporation must hire a secretary immediately, and the secretary must keep the minutes of all the organizational meetings.
    - The Secretary also states who is a shareholder of record at the time of the meeting.
    - **MBCA § 1.40(20):** "Secretary" means the corporate officer to whom the board of directors has delegated responsibility under section 8.40(c) for custody of the minutes of the meetings of the board of directors and of the shareholders and for authenticating records of the corporation.
- **Shareholders:**
  - In order for the corporation to start functioning, it needs MONEY!!! The corporation will turn to shareholders for that money.
  - **MBCA§ 6.21:** A person can become a shareholder once they pay for the consideration of the shares, and settlement must occur in 3 days.
  - Once a person purchases the shares, they do not immediately become a **shareholder of record**, the secretary must record it first.

- o Once the shareholder does become a shareholder of record, that shareholder can attend shareholder meetings.
- o You can also become a shareholder of record through a will or divorce.
    - This is not voluntary, but through operation of law—you step into that person who previously owned the shares and you have standing to sue.
- o **Meetings:**
    - How do shareholders of records, if they are corporations, attend shareholder meetings? Through a nominee.
    - **Nominee:** Creates a principal/agent relationship. The biological person attending the shareholder meeting on behalf of the corporation. The nominee has broader authority and can attend a shareholder meeting over a long period of time than a proxy.
    - **MBCA § 7.23 Shares held by Nominees:** A corporation may establish a procedure by which the beneficial owner of shares that are registered in the name of a nominee is recognized by the corporation as the shareholder. The extent of this recognition may be determined in the procedure.
    - Famous people/well-known investors who want to secure their identities will use nominees for privacy.
    - **Proxies:**
        - If I wanted to attend a shareholder meeting, but I am not on the record yet, how would I do so? I would need to get appointed as a proxy.
        - Who is a proxy?

- - - The proxy would be the agent going to the meeting on behalf of a corporation shareholder (principal) or a biological person shareholder (principal).
    - Typically, proxies take the place of shareholders of records for only one meeting, but it could be for more than one meeting if stated in a contract.
    - **MBCA § 7.22(d):** An appointment of a proxy is revocable UNLESS the appointment form or electronic transmission states that it is irrevocable and the appointment is coupled with an interest.
  - What is to prevent a corporation, such as E*Trade, from coming to the shareholder meeting for Nike?
    - If I, as a proxy for E*Trade, make a contract agreement with E*Trade, claiming that I am an irrevocable proxy, this would prevent E*Trade from coming to the Nike shareholder meeting.
  - **Receiver:** Is an irrevocable court-ordered proxy who will be allowed to attend the meeting, contrary to someone who may have been the original proxy attending shareholder meetings.
- **Types of Meetings:**

- Votes determine whether or not there is a meeting.
- **Annual Meeting:**
    - **MBCA § 7.01:** A corporation shall hold a meeting of shareholders annually at a time stated in or fixed in accordance with the bylaws.
    - The purpose of the first shareholder meeting is to vote in who will make up the corporation's board of directors.
    - The initial directors hold office until the first annul shareholder meeting, if no new directors are elected, the same initial directors stay on.
    - **MBCA § 8.05(a):** The terms of the initial directors of a corporation expire at the first shareholders' meeting at which directors are elected.
    - **The secretary of the corporation determines how many votes are present.**
    - **Notice of Annual Meeting:**
        - **MBCA § 7.05(a):** A corporations shall notify shareholders of the date, time, and place of each annual and special shareholders' meeting no fewer than 10 nor more than 60 days before the meeting date.

- **MBCA § 7.05(b):** Unless this statute or the articles of incorporation require otherwise, notice of an annual meeting need not include a description of the purpose or purposes for which the meeting is called.
- **Special Meeting:**
  - **MBCA § 7.02:** In order to hold a special meeting, there must be 10% of the holders entitled to cast votes, to call a special meeting. There MUST still be a quorum.
  - **The secretary of the corporation determines how many votes are present.**
  - **Notice of Special Meetings:**
    - **MBCA § 7.05:** A corporations shall notify shareholders of the date, time, and place of each annual and special shareholders' meeting no fewer than 10 nor more than 60 days before the meeting date.
    - **MBCA § 7.05(c):** Special meetings **MUST** include a description of purpose or purposes for which a special meeting is called.

- **Court Ordered Meeting:**
  - A meeting fixed by the court.
  - The court also determines the shares entitled to participate.
- **Shareholder Voting:**
  - **A shareholder quorum a majority of the votes present, however, even if the majority leaves, the votes remaining can still vote.**
  - **MBCA § 7.25(a): Quorum and Voting Requirements of Voting Groups:**
    - The meeting is legally in progress when a quorum is present. Shares entitled to vote as a separate voting group may take action on a matter at a meeting only if a quorum of those shares exists with respect to that matter. Unless the articles of incorporation provides otherwise, a majority of the votes entitled to be cast on the matter by the voting group constitutes a quorum of that voting group for action on that matter.
  - **Voting Agreement (coordinating votes):**
    - **MBCA § 7.31(a):** Two or more shareholders may provide for the manner in which they will vote their shares by signing an agreement for that purpose. A voting agreement created

- under this section is specifically enforceable.
- Make sure you tell your client to avoid deadlock when forming the board of directors.
- **Provisional Director:**
  - A court has the discretion to appoint a provisional director to serve the best interests of the corporation when deadlock arises.
- **Cumulative voting:**
  - Per share you get a number of votes, and you get to vote so if I own one share in Microsoft and have 4 votes, then I can add my votes up and place them all for one person. Number shares times the number of slots open=how many votes you get (1 share x 4 positions open you are voting on=4 votes).
- **Straight Voting:**
  - The acting of using one's shares to vote for a person in the same way.
  - So if I have 4 shares, I will use my 4 shares to vote for one person (or vote in one way).

33

- **Shareholder Agreements:**
  - Using section 7.32, using a spectrum, using one extreme pool, the shareholders could agree to eliminate the board of directors all together and the shareholders would manage the corporation. This would be more like a corporation family. This is similar to agreements in corporate tax.
  - Who would need to be parties to section 7.32? Using 7.32, the shareholders can do something inconsistent with the Model Business Corp. Act.
  - 7.32 allows you to break a deadlock if you have to.
- **Publically Traded Corporations:**
  - Example: Apple
  - Large corporations are publically traded.
  - These are corps of a certain size regulated by federal law, by the securities act 1933 and 1934, and they must be registered by the securities act of 1933 because the federal gov. is going to make sure that these corps. do not steal money from the public.
- **Closely Held Corporations:**
  - This type of corporation gets money from shareholders by first making an offer to the people to purchase shares on credit or cash.
  - The general public is not allowed to buy shares.
  - The articles of incorporation will determine whether or not the corporation is closed or open.
  - **Closed corporations tend to be smaller and tax law permits the closed corporation to be subchapter S and avoid having to pay corporate tax, in which**

case the corporation would be treated as a partnership.
- **MBCA § 6.27:** The articles of incorporation put restriction on the transfer of shares.
  - Restrictions such as, first right of refusal.
- **Ultra Vires:**
  - An ultra vires act occurs when one commits an act that is beyond the powers or purpose of the corporation.
  - The legislature has stepped in and these contracts the corporation has formed, though outside of the corporation's initial purpose as stated in the corporation's articles of incorporation, are VALID, BINDING, AND ENFORCEABLE, despite the ultra vires doctrine.
  - Therefore, if No Name Shoes decides to sell both shoes and hot dogs and contracts with Utopia Hot Dog Buns, then No Name Shoes cannot hide behind their purpose of only selling shoes so that the other businesses No Name Shoes contracts with cannot sue No Name Shoes if it defaults on its contract.
- **Characteristics of a Closely-Held Corporation:**
  - 1. The restrictions in the articles.
  - 2. Small number of shareholders in the particular corporation.
  - 3. We want to avoid deadlock in the management.
- **Liability of the Corporation:**
  - **MBCA § 6.22: Liability of Shareholders:**

- Unless otherwise provided in the articles of incorporation, a shareholder of a corporation is not personally liable for the acts or debts of the corporation except that he may become personally liable by reason of his own acts or conduct.
- This limits liability of the members in the corporation.
- **Courts will impose unlimited personal liability on the shareholders of the corporation when any of these are proven:**
  - **1. Fraud**
  - **2. Illegality**
  - **3. Failure to comply with the corporate statute**
    - If any of the shareholder of the corporation appear to act as if they are operating a sole proprietorship, then the court may impose unlimited personal liability.
    - ***Dewitt Truck Brokers v. W. Ray Flemming Fruit Co.***
      - The Corp. never had corporate records, a stockholders meeting, no separate bank account between the business and personal bank account, and no payment of dividends, and the court imposed unlimited personal liability on the

corporation because the corporation was operating as a sole proprietorship.
- Corporate Books and Records
  - **MBCA § 16.01(a):** requires every corporate to **_keep_** as permanent records a minimum set of core documents that reflect decisions made by the directors and shareholders of the corporation.
  - **MBCA § 16.01(e):** requires every corporate to keep a copy of specified basic corporate documents at the principal office of the corporation (**_maintain_**). These documents must be available for routine inspection by any shareholder during regular business hours **MBCA § 16.02(a).**
  - **MBCA § 16.01(b):** requires every corporation to **_maintain appropriate_** accounting records. Also, the nature and size of the business largely determines the corporation's accounting system, which in turn largely determines its accounting records.
    - **There is a difference between maintain and keep.**
      - **Keep:** means permanent retention, while
      - **Maintain:** refers to current records only and does not address the question of how long financial and other records should be kept.
  - **MBCA § 16.01(c):** requires every corporation to "**_maintain_**" a record of its shareholders. In larger corporations, records

of shareholders are usually maintained electronically.
- **Shareholder Entitlements:**
  - A shareholder is entitled to a bundle of rights under **MBCA § 16.02(b):**
    - A shareholder of a corporation is entitled to inspect and copy, during regular business hours at a reasonable location specified by the corporation, any of the following records of the corporation if the shareholder meets the requirements of subsection (c) and gives the corporation written notice of his demand at least 5 business days before the date on which he wishes to inspect and copy.
    - **What triggers inspection rights (3 elements)?**
      - 1. MBCA § 16.02(c)(1):
        - **(a) Good Faith:**
          - Good faith is presumed by virtue of a shareholder making a demand—a rebuttable presumption.
          - The burden shifts to the corporation to prove the shareholder's demand was not made in good

faith, if challenged.
- **(b) Proper Purpose:**
  - The proper purpose for the inspection of the corporation's records must be reasonably related to the shareholder's interest.
  - The primary purpose must be proper, and other secondary purposes will be irrelevant.
- **2. Reasonably Particularity:**
  - Shareholder must list in writing the particularities of his or her purpose.
  - Shareholder must list specific instances/facts supporting her conclusory statements.
  - The shareholder must list enough information so that a reasonable person would know what the shareholder is referring to.
- **3. Connected Records:**
  - The records are directly connected with the shareholder's purpose.

- **Board of Directors:**
    - Each corporation MUST have a board of directors.
    - 100% of corporate powers shall be exercised or under the authority of the board of directors of the corporation.
    - **Articles of Incorporation:**
    - **Directors & Officers of a Closely Held Corporation:**
        - **MBCA § 8.01(a):** Except as provided in section 7.32, each corporation must have a board of directors.
        - This is important because of section **(b) of 8.01:**
            - All corporate powers SHALL be exercised by or under the authority of the board of directors of the corporation, and the business and affairs of the corporation shall be managed by or under the direction and subject to the oversight, or its boards of directors, subject to any limitations set forth in the articles of incorporation or in an agreement authorized under section 7.32.
        - However, the legislature acknowledges that in the context of business, the legislature is essentially hands off, and permits, those who are informed and experienced to organize the smaller, closed corporation as how shareholders see fit.
        - This allows the shareholders to used the articles of incorporation to manage the corporation as they see fit.
        - Or the shareholders can use section 7.32 to make agreements as the shareholders sees fit.

- Directors Meetings:
  - **How do the board of directors function if the corporation has directors under section 8.01?**
    - Board of directors have meeting just as shareholders have meetings.
    - Board of directors can have regular or special meetings. 2-types, but courts can also order court order meetings.
    - The board of directors can only be biological persons.
      - **Section 8.22(a) Regular Meetings:** Unless the articles of incorporation or bylaws provide otherwise, regular meetings of the board of directors may be held WITHOUT notice of the date, time, place, or purpose of the meeting.
      - **Section 8.22(b) Special Meetings:** Unless the articles of incorporation or bylaws provide for a longer or shorter period, special meetings of the boards of directors must be preceded by at least 2 days notice. The notice need not describe the purpose of the special meeting unless required by the articles of incorporation or bylaws.
      - **MBCA § 8.23: Waiver of Notice:** A director may waive any notice required by this Act, the articles of incorporation, or

bylaws or after the date and time stated in the notice. Except as provided by (b), the waiver must be in writing, signed by the director entitled to the notice, and filed with the minutes or corporate records.
- **Voting:**
  - **Director Quorum:**
    - A meeting is **_LEGALLY UNDERWAY_** when there is a quorum present.
    - In order for a meeting of directors to be underway, a quorum is necessary.
    - A is quorum present when there is a majority of the board of directors.
- **Director Management Control:**
  - The board of directors decide who the officers of the corporation will be.
  - **How would that decision me made?**
    - The board of the directors meeting is in progress.
  - **How is it that the particular person fulfills the position?**
    - One of the board of the directors tells the board that they have an agent.
    - A proposal would be made, and another board of directors would second that proposal.
- **Duty of Care & Business Judgment Rule:**
  - **MBCA § 8.30(a):** The directors shall act (1) in good faith and (2) in a manner the directors reasonably believes to be in the best interests of the corporation.
  - **What are the board of directors empowered to do under corporate law,**

and what are the limitation, and what are the ways the board of directors can be held liable?
- In what circumstances would the board of directors be subject to liability?
  - 1. Fraud. Section 8.09(a)
    - If the director engaged in fraudulent conduct with respect to the corporation or its shareholders, grossly abused the position of director or intentionally inflicted harm on the corporation.
    - The burden of proof rests of the party claiming the director or directors committed a fraudulent act.
  - 2. Illegal Conduct
  - 3. Breach of Fiduciary Duty,
    - Examples:
      - (a) Negligence
      - (b) Actions NOT in good faith
- **Business Judgment Rule:** It is a rebuttable presumption, as it is presumed to be informed, but the judgment will not be shielded under the rule if the judgment is unadvised.
  - The courts give the board of directors discretion because it is presumed that they are acting with good faith on behalf of the corporation.

- The court will look to see if the board was reasonably informed prior to making the decision.
- By reasonable, the court will look what material information a reasonable person would want to have before reaching that decision.
- The issue of whether the board was reasonably informed prior to making this decision for the presumption of the business judgment rule to be in place is a question of fact.
- The reasonableness is based on the objective test of a reasonable person.
- Board of directors=guardian ad litem
- Corporation=disabled child
- Shareholders=family members

- **Derivative Suits:**
  - **Standing:**
    - **MBCA § 7.41:** A shareholder may not commence or maintain a derivative proceeding unless the shareholder:
      - **(1)** was a shareholder of the corporation at the time of the act or omission complained of or become a shareholder through transfer by operation of law from one who was a shareholder at that time.
    - In order to file a derivative suit, you must be a shareholder of record on the date of the derivative suit.
    - However, you can also establish that you are a shareholder of record on the date of the derivative suit if you are the beneficiary to a will.

- **Universal Demand State:**
  - **MBCA § 7.42:**
    - No shareholder may commence a derivative proceeding until:
      - (1) a written demand has been made upon the corporation to take suitable action; and
      - (2) 90 days have expired from the date the demand was made unless the shareholder has earlier been notified that the demand has been rejected by the corporation or unless irreparable injury to the corporation would result by waiting for the expiration of the 90-day period.
    - (A) The board of directors stated that they refuse to go further with the demand in 90 days.
    - (B) Or the board of the directors have not responded to the demand, and after 90 days expired.
    - (C) (Shareholder would allege that) The corporation would suffer irreparable harm if action is not taken right away.
- **Demand Futility (Demand-Excused States):**
  - This is NOT a universal demand state.
  - In these states, the shareholders do not have to send a demand to the corporation if they can present the court with appropriate circumstances where demands can be excused.
  - Demand futility will apply in situations where the board sues themselves as biological

persons. People are not that honest, and that impartial—that a human would file suit against themselves.
- **Special Litigation Committee:**
  - Once a derivate suit is filed, the board of directors will place together a special litigation committee, to determine whether the derivative suit is or is not in the corporation's best interests.
  - The court will exercise its discretion in granting summary judgment in favor of the board of directors, or whether a motion to dismiss with prejudice so that liability is imposed on no one and the matter is adjudicated on no one.
  - OR the court may dismiss the suit without prejudice.
  - In any event, it depends on the SLC as to what course of action the court takes.
  - What side the courts come down on also depends on who made up the SLC.
  - **1. The SLC must be independent.**
  - **2. The SLC that they conducted a reasonable inquiry in depth.**
  - **3. The inquiry must also be in good faith.**
  - **If the court was persuaded that the committee was independent, acted in good faith and made a reasonable inquiry, then if the SLC passes muster, then the court may very well dismiss the derivative suit.**
  - If the corporation is making a motion to dismiss, what is corporate law's position for whom the burden of proof rests?

- **The corporation!! The corporation is the moving party requesting the motion to dismiss.**
- In what circumstances, would the court dismiss the suit?
    - The burden of proof is on the moving party, which is the corporation.
    - **Alternative A:** When the demand came into the corporation under 7.42, the directors might have held a meeting to determine if there were any independent directors, and if the independent directors held a meeting and had voted in favor of not bringing the action, that is one alternative.
        - **This is not the best alternative.**
    - **Alternative B:** Even if under B there are not enough independent directors as in A, consisting exclusively of independent directors, might the SLC still go ahead and vote and decide that no corporate action be brought.
    - **Alternative C:** The directors might decide to put together a SLC in place, if there are enough independent directors to decide to put in place a SLC consisting of independent committee members, then arguably, this is what the independent directors would do.
    - **Alternative D:** If the board went ahead and created an SLC anyway, but the board who created that SLC were not independent. What would be the court's reaction under D to a SLC

47

put in place by the board members who are not independent. What if the board empowered the SLC to conduct a special determination would arise, are the committee members acting in good faith, and the nature.
- **Which alternative would be treated with the greatest respect by the court in deciding whether to dismiss the derivative action or not.**
    o Alternative C because of the impartiality of the special litigation committee and because the committee was selected by a body of independent directors.
- **The Court will dismiss the derivative suit if the board is independent, selects an independent committee, and the committee conducts an inquiry that passes muster, that was broad enough, conducted in good faith, and was reasonable.**
- **This power rests with the court in the court's discretion because the court is really using the fact that the committee was independent.**
    o **Intrinsic Fairness Test:**
        ▪ The initial burden of proof is on the shareholder bringing the suit because the shareholder would essentially be the nominal plaintiff.
        ▪ Once the shareholder has provide its burden of self-dealing, then the burden of proof

shifts to the board of directors to prove that their actions were intrinsically fair to the corporation.
- A director that enters into a self-dealing transaction has the burden of showing that the transaction is intrinsically fair to the corporation.
- Meaning the terms of the transaction are fair and reasonable, and that the director has not used his or her position to take advantage of the corporation.

- **Presidential Power:**
  - The president only has apparent authority to bind her company by acts arising in the usual and regular course of business but NOT for contracts of an "extraordinary nature."
  - Whether apparent authority exists is a question of fact.
  - The President's power can either be found in the articles of incorporation, the bylaws, the state statutes, contract law, or if all these avenues are silent, then we look to trade custom and trade usage.
  - The president's power in a particular industry in a particular controversy in a particular corporation is a question of fact. It would be based on a reasonable president acting in the same or similar industry.
  - **Apparent Authority is essentially a question of fact, it depends not only on these factors:**
    - The nature of the contract involved, but the officer negotiating it.
    - The corporation's usual manner of conducting business, the size of the corporation and the number of its stockholders,
    - The circumstances that give rise to the contract,
    - The reasonableness of the contract, the among involved, and
    - Who the contracting third party is.

- You could also allow the President to do what the board of directors do, such as hire officers. You could prove this by presenting evidence of a course of dealing

Made in the USA
San Bernardino, CA
10 October 2018